DISCLAIMER

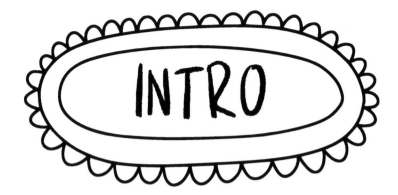

INTRO

No one can really prepare you for motherhood, even with all the advice from friends, family and the good old internet.

The thing I was most unprepared for was raising my kids in a society that is so heavily focused on electronics, and social media. Our kids are confronted with bullying, comparison, and mental health struggles, now more than ever before.

When my oldest was 5, I enrolled her into Sparks through Girl Guides of Canada. It didn't take long before I became a leader for my daughter's Sparks unit and started planning for our year. What I loved about the program was that I got to be a part of empowering young girls to challenge themselves, build confidence and have fun along the way of finding their true authentic selves.

But being a leader opened my eyes to just how many kids are struggling to deal with their feelings. Even worse, in most settings they have a lack of access to the resources they need to work through them.

Fast forward a few years and my daughter got into grade five. She felt lost around that time of her life, trying to figure out who she was and where she fit in. To make it worse she was being bullied by a group of girls and that took a toll on her health. She dealt with anxiety, hair loss, and loss of sleep.

With the help of a child therapist, keeping an open line of communication, and using different tools I have discovered on my own personal journey, my daughter has been able to start working through the challenges she is facing in a healthy way.

This experience of being a mother and raising my daughter is what inspired me to create this workbook. I know that if these are challenges that my children have to go through, that many other children have to go through the same challenges every day.
Every child is different in their own unique way and as mothers, we want to embrace that.

I believe we can help our children process what they're feeling in a mature and healthy way. That way, kids can grow up happier, more confident in themselves and step into adulthood with their best foot forward.
I feel in my heart that it's small steps like this that make a big impact with kids today, and that is why I wanted to write this workbook.
Just like my own kids, more than anything I want your kids to be happy. I want them to feel like they can be true to their authentic selves, and lead by example to make this world happier.

I hope this 20 day challenge workbook helps your child feel empowered, understood, and gives them the tools they need to live their best life.

BRITTANY HARPER
MOM AND CHILDREN'S MENTAL HEALTH ADVOCATE

20
EXERCISES

DAY 1:

WRITE TO YOUR FUTURE SELF

Writing a letter to your future self is a powerful exercise. It's a chance to capture your current thoughts, dreams, and goals, and then send them into the future to see how much you've grown and changed.

Now, you might be thinking, "Why the heck am I writing a letter to my future self?"

Well, life can feel like a rollercoaster of emotions and experiences, and this letter allows you to freeze a moment in time. It's an opportunity to reflect on your hopes, fears, and aspirations, and to set intentions for the person you want to become.

When you receive this letter years from now, you'll have a chance to connect with your younger self, gain perspective on your journey, and celebrate the progress you've made.

So, take this moment to express yourself honestly, and don't be afraid to dream big and embrace the uncertainty that comes with growing up. Your future self will thank you for it.

Bonus tip: Save this letter and come back to it in a year from now to see how much you've grown.

DEAR FUTURE ME,

LOVE FROM,

DAY 2:

♡ SELF FORGIVENESS ♡

Self-forgiveness is like giving a warm hug to yourself when you've made a mistake or done something you wish you hadn't.

It means understanding that everyone makes errors sometimes, and that's completely okay. Just like how you forgive your friends when they make mistakes, you can also forgive yourself. It's a way of being kind to yourself and letting go of the heavy feelings that come with guilt or sadness.

Forgiving yourself can lead to better emotional wellbeing, healthier relationships, positive behavioral changes, and overall higher levels of satisfaction and self-compassion.

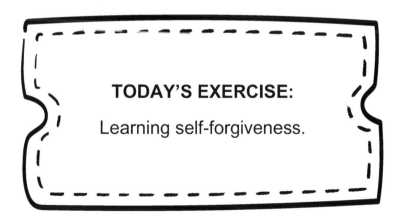

TODAY'S EXERCISE:

Learning self-forgiveness.

Set aside a few moments to recall instances when you've been self-critical or uttered negative statements to yourself. Answer the following journal prompts:

TODAY I FORGIVE MYSELF FOR

———————————————————

———————————————————

———————————————————

IN ORDER TO MOVE ON, I ACKNOWLEDGE THAT I WAS WRONG IN HOW I

———————————————————

———————————————————

———————————————————

I DESERVE FORGIVENESS BECAUSE

_____

_____

_____

_____

NEXT TIME I AM FACED WITH A SIMILAR
DECISION I WILL

_____

_____

_____

_____

DAY 3:

LEARNING TO FORGIVE OTHERS

Who hasn't been hurt by the actions or words of another?

It's unfair, but it happens. Forgiving someone doesn't mean that they never did anything wrong. Forgiving someone means that you love yourself enough to let go of certain situations that no longer serve you.

This exercise is to help you let go of negative emotions that are holding you down from past experiences.

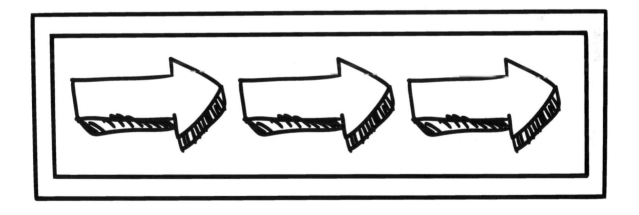

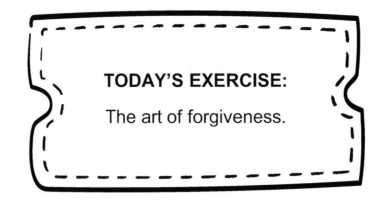

TODAY'S EXERCISE:

The art of forgiveness.

Write down 5-10 instances when someone treated you unkindly.

ONE: _____.

TWO: _____.

THREE: _____.

FOUR: _____.

FIVE: _____.

Take a moment to reflect on why they might have behaved that way on those particular days. Consider what could have been happening in their own lives that led them to act unkindly. Regardless of their reasons, it's essential to acknowledge that you have the power to release the hurt you feel associated with these memories.

Take a deep breath in, and as you exhale say out loud:

"As I let go of this hurt, I choose to forgive [Name]. I release the hold this pain has had on me. I am choosing peace and healing. I am free to move forward and create a better future for myself."

Make a conscious choice to forgive them and move forward. Repeat this process for each of the moments you've recalled.

DAY 4:

AFFIRM WHO YOU ARE

Affirming who you are is a powerful act of self-recognition and self-love. It's a journey of embracing your unique qualities, acknowledging your strengths, and embracing your flaws as part of your beautiful tapestry.

When you affirm who you are, you give yourself permission to be authentic, to follow your passions, and to chase your dreams with unwavering determination. It's a declaration that your worth is not determined by external opinions or societal standards, but by the love and acceptance you hold for yourself.

In this act of affirmation, you pave the way for personal growth, resilience, and a life lived with purpose and authenticity.

TODAY'S EXERCISE:

My positive points.

On the sticky notes, write down three positive statements that describe the person you aspire to become. Put these sticky notes in places around your home that you frequently visit, such as your bathroom or bedroom. Whenever you come across one of these sticky notes, say the statement out loud with confidence, reaffirming your goals and intentions.

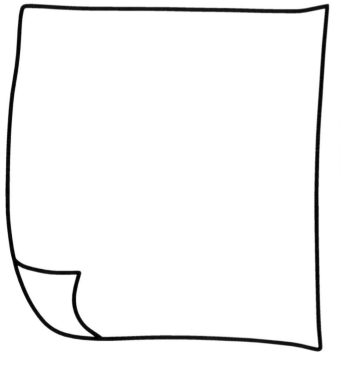

DAY 5:

BREATHWORK FOR STRESS RELIEF

Breathwork can be a powerful tool especially when paired with powerful visualization techniques like in today's exercise. By practicing breathwork regularly, you can maintain a sense of calm and balance in your life.

You can use deep breathing either throughout the day, when you're feeling overwhelmed or anxious, need to relax or go to sleep, to calm your body after exercising, or even just to pause and reset.

TODAY'S EXERCISE:

Deep breathing.

Visualize an infinity symbol and trace the symbol with one finger while breathing in and out. This can be a helpful tool to achieve a smooth and even breath cycle. Inhale as you follow one half of the symbol and exhale as they follow the other half.

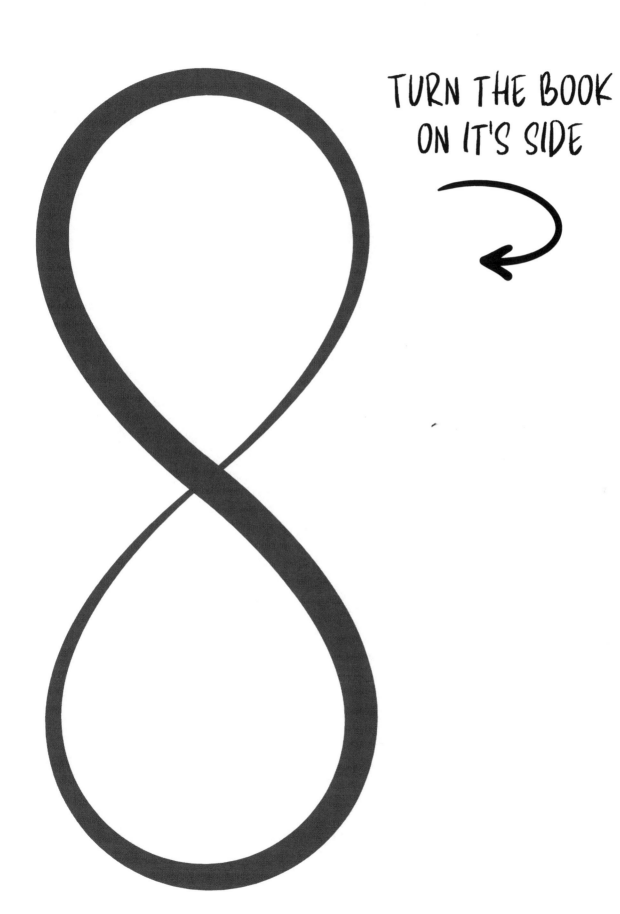

TURN THE BOOK
ON IT'S SIDE

DAY 6:

GRATITUDE

When you embrace gratitude, you open your heart to the beauty of the present moment and acknowledge the support and love you receive from others.

Oftentimes, when you're in a bad mood, it's because you're focused on the bad. Gratitude strengthens your relationships, and encourages you to appreciate the people who bring positivity into your life. This can instantly improve your mood.

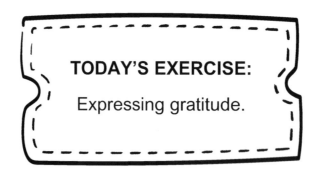

TODAY'S EXERCISE:

Expressing gratitude.

Find a quiet spot and set a timer for 1 minute. When the timer begins, verbally express your gratitude for as many things as possible. Be creative and think beyond what's obvious.

EX) "I'm grateful for my hands because they allow me to play my favorite sport."

Keep expressing what you're grateful for without pausing until the entire minute has passed.

DAY 7:

LETTING GO OF NEGATIVE FEELINGS

Releasing negative feelings is an important skill because it allows you to maintain your emotional well-being and build healthier relationships. Holding onto negativity can be emotionally draining and even harmful to your mental and physical health.

To release negative feelings, you need to acknowledge and understand them. This means identifying what's causing these emotions, whether it's an event, a thought, or an interaction with someone else.

Once you've pinpointed the source, you can work on finding constructive ways to express and process these emotions. This might involve talking to someone you trust, engaging in activities that make us feel better, or using relaxation techniques.

Releasing negative feelings helps us let go of unnecessary burdens and move towards a more positive and peaceful state of mind.

TODAY'S EXERCISE:

Releasing negative
emotions.

Think about any negative emotions you may be experiencing towards yourself or someone else, such as anger, sadness, or any troubling feelings.

Locate a leaf from the ground, or if one isn't available, draw a leaf on a piece of paper.

Express those negative emotions by writing or drawing them on the leaf. This act helps you externalize these emotions.

Step outside, take a deep breath, and envision yourself releasing those emotions. Imagine the wind carrying them away as you let go of the leaf. If you used paper, dispose of it in a secure manner or find an appropriate place to discard it. If you used a real leaf, gently return it to nature.

Take a moment to contemplate how you feel after releasing those negative emotions. Do you sense a lightness or increased peace within you? Make note of your observations.

DAY 8:

CREATE A VISION OF YOUR FUTURE

Creating a vision of your future is an exciting and empowering step as you grow older. It's like painting a picture of the life you want to live.

Start by imagining where you see yourself in the future—what kind of person you want to become, what you want to achieve, and what makes you truly happy. Setting goals and working towards them will be a big part of your journey.

Remember, it's okay if your vision changes along the way; life is full of surprises and new opportunities. The important thing is to stay focused, stay true to yourself, and keep taking steps towards the future you dream of.

Your future is yours to create, and the possibilities are endless!

TODAY'S EXERCISE:

Visualization.

Close your eyes and take a few deep breaths. Imagine yourself in one year from now. How old will you be? What do you want your life to be like at that time?

Write about the kind of person you want to grow up to be. Think about qualities like kindness, courage, determination, and anything else you admire in others.

Consider what you want to achieve or experience in the next year. What are your dreams and goals? This could be being on a sports team, joining a band, or anything else you'd like to accomplish. Write down the things you're striving towards.

Take all your thoughts and visions and create a picture or a collage to represent your dreams for the next year. Use pictures from magazines or print photos off that you find online. This will be your dream board.

Keep this dream board in a special place where you can see it often. It will serve as a reminder of your goals and dreams for the future. Remember that dreams can change as you grow, and that's okay. You can do this exercise every year to update your dreams and see how you've grown.

MY DREAM BOARD

DAY 9:

EASING ANXIETY

Learning to ease anxiety is a valuable skill that will serve you well as you navigate the challenges and adventures of your life.

It involves recognizing when you're feeling anxious, understanding your thoughts and feelings that trigger your anxiety, and then employing various strategies to manage it. Techniques like deep breathing, mindfulness, and positive self-talk can be incredibly effective in calming anxious thoughts. Additionally, finding healthy outlets for stress through activities you enjoy, such as hobbies, sports, or creative pursuits can help alleviate anxiety.

Remember, it's okay to seek support from trusted adults, teachers, or counselors if you ever feel overwhelmed.

TODAY'S EXERCISE:

Exploring ways to calm anxiety and feel less worried.

Today, you'll explore ways to calm anxiety and feel less worried. This exercise will help you feel more in control of your feelings and find ways to manage anxiety.

In a journal, write out your answers to the following questions:

WHAT IS MAKING ME ANXIOUS?

_____

_____

_____

_____

_____

_____

_____

_____

WHAT ARE SOME OF THE NEGATIVE THOUGHTS I AM HAVING? (NAME 3)

1) _____

2) _____

3) _____

HOW IS MY BODY RESPONDING?

_____

_____

_____

_____

_____

_____

WHAT IS THE WORST THING THAT CAN HAPPEN?

_____

_____

_____

_____

_____

_____

_____

_____

_____

WHAT DO I HAVE IN MY CONTROL TO KEEP THIS FROM HAPPENING?

_____

_____

_____

_____

_____

_____

_____

_____

_____

WHAT CAN I DO TO CALM DOWN?

―――――――――――――――――――――

―――――――――――――――――――――

―――――――――――――――――――――

―――――――――――――――――――――

―――――――――――――――――――――

―――――――――――――――――――――

―――――――――――――――――――――

―――――――――――――――――――――

―――――――――――――――――――――

―――――――――――――――――――――

WHAT ARE POSITIVE THOUGHTS TO HELP CALM MY MIND?

_____

_____

_____

_____

_____

_____

_____

_____

_____

DAY 10:

STAYING TRUE TO YOURSELF BY CONQUERING PEER PRESSURE

Staying true to yourself in the face of peer pressure is a courageous and empowering act of self-discovery.

In a world where conformity often seems like the easier path, it takes inner strength and self-awareness to resist the pull of external influences. Conquering peer pressure means recognizing your values, beliefs, and aspirations and having the confidence to uphold them, even when those around you may be pushing in a different direction. It's a reminder that your individuality is a source of strength, not weakness.

By staying true to yourself, you not only maintain your integrity, but also become a role model for others who may be struggling with the same pressures.

It's a journey of self-respect and authenticity that leads to a life guided by your own principles and a sense of fulfillment that can't be found by simply following the crowd.

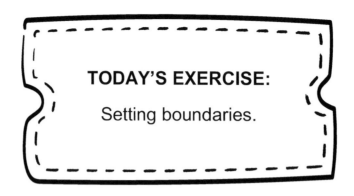

TODAY'S EXERCISE:

Setting boundaries.

Think about a time when you faced peer pressure, and your friends wanted you to do something you didn't feel comfortable with. It could be something you experienced recently or in the past.

Write about that situation, describing how you stayed true to yourself. What did you do, and how did you feel afterward?

Consider the choices you made that felt right for you. Write down some ways you can keep making choices that align with who you are. For example:

Set boundaries: Know your limits and be clear about what you're comfortable with.

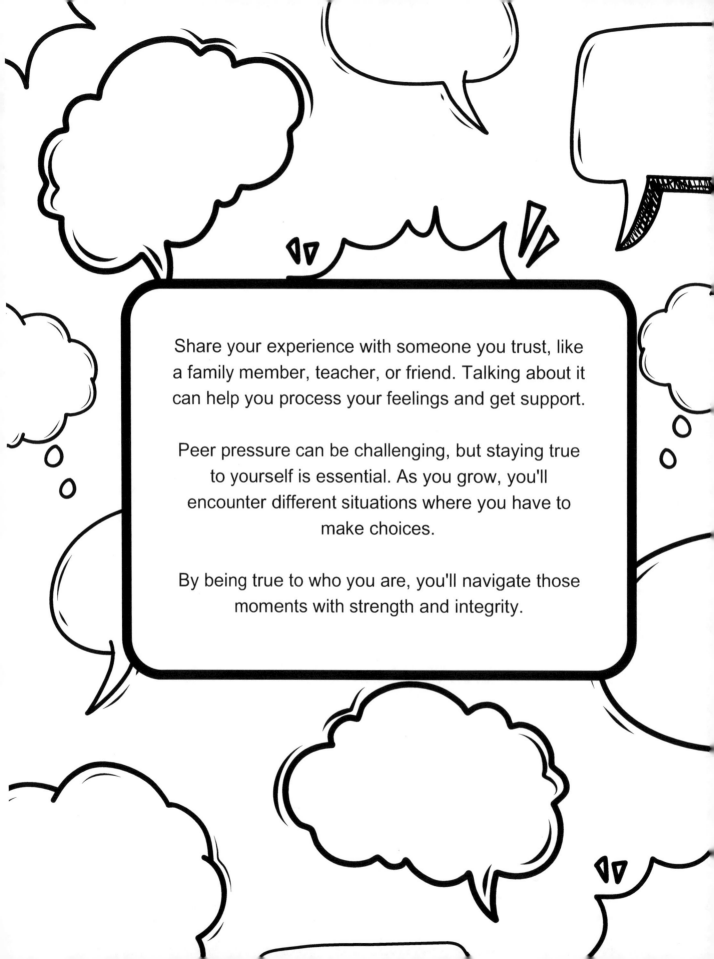

Share your experience with someone you trust, like a family member, teacher, or friend. Talking about it can help you process your feelings and get support.

Peer pressure can be challenging, but staying true to yourself is essential. As you grow, you'll encounter different situations where you have to make choices.

By being true to who you are, you'll navigate those moments with strength and integrity.

DAY 11:

PUTTING AN END TO BULLYING!

In this activity, you will explore strategies to combat bullying and support those who may be affected by it.

The goal is to promote kindness and improve your school environment, ensuring it's safe and welcoming for everyone. It's crucial to know who you can turn to if you witness bullying.

We'll take a moment to consider the harmful impact of bullying on others and empathize with how it might feel if you or someone you care about were a victim of bullying.

TODAY'S EXERCISE:

What can you do?

List ways in which you can intervene to stop bullying or assist someone facing it.

EX) Confide in a trusted adult, like a teacher, school counselor, or parent, and report the bullying.

Think about actions you can take to contribute to a more positive school atmosphere.

_____

_____

_____

_____

_____

_____

_____

_____

_____

Write down ways to spread kindness and create an environment where respect and care thrive.

_____

_____

_____

_____

_____

_____

_____

_____

_____

_____

_____

Share your ideas with your classmates or friends, and encourage them to join you in cultivating a more compassionate and respectful school community.

Consider identifying trusted adults or friends you can reach out to if you witness bullying, and make a list of these individuals who can provide help and support when needed.

—————————————————————————————

—————————————————————————————

—————————————————————————————

—————————————————————————————

—————————————————————————————

—————————————————————————————

—————————————————————————————

—————————————————————————————

—————————————————————————————

DAY 12:

LOVE THE SKIN YOU'RE IN

Being body positive is about building a healthy and accepting relationship with your body.

It means recognizing that bodies come in all shapes and sizes, and that's what makes each person unique. Instead of fixating on appearances, focus on nourishing and taking care of your body for the sake of feeling healthy and strong. Embrace self-love and self-acceptance by celebrating what your body can do, whether it's dancing, playing sports, or simply being resilient in challenging times.

Body positivity is about appreciating your body for all the incredible things it enables you to experience in life and understanding that your worth is not determined by how you look, but by who you are as a person.

TODAY'S EXERCISE:

Loving myself.

Think about the things you like about yourself that have nothing to do with how you look. It could be your kindness, sense of humor, intelligence, creativity, or any other inner qualities you appreciate.

Write down those qualities that you love about yourself. Celebrate these traits and remember they make you unique and special.

Focus on these inner qualities and think about how they define you more than your appearance. Embrace them as essential parts of who you are.

_____

_____

_____

_____

_____

_____

_____

_____

_____

Reflect on how taking care of yourself can lead to greater confidence.
Write activities you can do to practice self-care, such as:

EX) Engaging in physical activities that make you feel strong and healthy.

—————————————————————————————

—————————————————————————————

—————————————————————————————

—————————————————————————————

—————————————————————————————

—————————————————————————————

—————————————————————————————

—————————————————————————————

—————————————————————————————

—————————————————————————————

DAY 13:

BOOSTING SELF-ESTEEM

In this activity, you'll explore what makes you feel good about yourself. You'll discover ways to engage in those positive activities more often and learn how saying positive things to yourself can boost your self-esteem.

This exercise will help you promote self-confidence and develop a positive self-image through self-affirmations and engaging in activities that uplift you. Boosting your self-esteem is essential for a healthy and happy life. Embrace the things that make you feel good about yourself, and don't forget to remind yourself of your worth through positive affirmations.

TODAY'S EXERCISE:

What makes me feel good about myself.

Think about what makes you feel good about yourself. It could be achieving a goal, helping others, making someone smile, learning new things, or anything else that brings you joy and a sense of accomplishment.

Write down those things that boost your self-esteem. Celebrate these moments and recognize your worth in accomplishing them.

Consider how you can do these activities more often to enhance your self-esteem. Write down steps you can take to engage in these positive experiences regularly.

Practice saying positive things to yourself to boost your self-esteem. Write down some self-affirmations you can say each day, such as:

"I am proud of myself for trying new things."

———————————————————————

———————————————————————

———————————————————————

———————————————————————

———————————————————————

Reflect on how repeating these positive statements can help you feel more confident and capable. Commit to saying them to yourself regularly to build a strong sense of self.

DAY 14:

EMBRACING YOUR OUTWARD IDENTITY

Today, you'll explore your identity by understanding your interests and beliefs. You'll discover ways to express who you really are and find acceptance by learning more about yourself and connecting with like-minded people.

The purpose of this exercise is to promote self-discovery, self-expression, and finding a supportive community that embraces your true self. By being true to who you are and seeking out a supportive community, you'll feel more confident and accepted in expressing your true self.

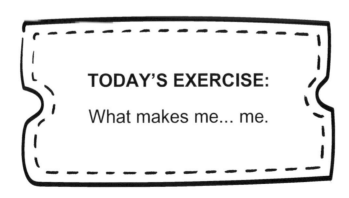

TODAY'S EXERCISE:

What makes me... me.

Reflect on the things you're interested in or strongly believe in. It could be your hobbies, favorite subjects, causes you care about, or anything that brings you joy and passion.

Write down those interests and beliefs that define your identity. Celebrate these aspects and acknowledge how they make you unique.

Consider ways you can show who you really are to the world. Write down how you can express your interests and beliefs, such as:

EX) Sharing your thoughts and ideas with friends, family, or online communities.

Think about how you can learn more about yourself. Write down activities you can do for self-discovery, such as:

EX) Keeping a journal to explore your thoughts and feelings.

—————————————————————————————

—————————————————————————————

—————————————————————————————

—————————————————————————————

—————————————————————————————

—————————————————————————————

—————————————————————————————

—————————————————————————————

—————————————————————————————

—————————————————————————————

Reflect on finding people who accept you for who you are. Write down ways you can connect with like-minded individuals, such as:

EX) Joining clubs or groups with shared interests.

—————————————————————————

—————————————————————————

—————————————————————————

—————————————————————————

—————————————————————————

—————————————————————————

—————————————————————————

—————————————————————————

—————————————————————————

—————————————————————————

DAY 15:

NURTURING POSITIVE FRIENDSHIPS

By nurturing open communication and appreciating desirable friend qualities, you'll create stronger and more fulfilling connections with those around you.

Positive friendships require effort and understanding from both sides. This exercise aims to promote healthy and fulfilling friendships. You'll explore ways to make your friendships stronger and more positive.

You'll learn how to communicate your feelings and resolve conflicts with friends, and you'll identify the qualities you look for in a good friend.

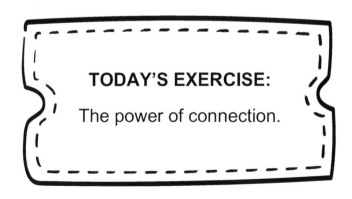

TODAY'S EXERCISE:

The power of connection.

Reflect on your friendships and think about ways to make them stronger and more positive. Write down some ideas to nurture these connections, such as:

EX) Listen actively when your friends share their thoughts and feelings.

_____

_____

_____

_____

_____

_____

_____

_____

_____

_____

Consider how you can talk about your feelings and solve problems when conflicts arise with your friends. Write down ways to communicate effectively, such as:

EX) Listen to your friend's perspective and try to understand their feelings too.

—— —— —— —— —— —— —— —— —— —— —— —— —— —— ——

—— —— —— —— —— —— —— —— —— —— —— —— —— —— ——

—— —— —— —— —— —— —— —— —— —— —— —— —— —— ——

—— —— —— —— —— —— —— —— —— —— —— —— —— —— ——

—— —— —— —— —— —— —— —— —— —— —— —— —— —— ——

—— —— —— —— —— —— —— —— —— —— —— —— —— —— ——

—— —— —— —— —— —— —— —— —— —— —— —— —— —— ——

—— —— —— —— —— —— —— —— —— —— —— —— —— —— ——

—— —— —— —— —— —— —— —— —— —— —— —— —— —— ——

—— —— —— —— —— —— —— —— —— —— —— —— —— —— ——

Think about the qualities you value in a friend. Write the characteristics you look for, such as:

EX)
- *Trustworthy*
- *loyal*

Reflect on how you can be a good friend to others by embodying these qualities. Write down ways to be the friend you want to have.

_____

_____

_____

_____

_____

_____

_____

_____

_____

_____

_____

DAY 16:

EXPLORING YOUR INWARD IDENTITY

Exploring your inward identity can be an exciting and transformative journey.

It's a time when you begin to ask questions about who you are and what makes you unique. It's about discovering your passions, values, and beliefs, and understanding how they shape your thoughts and actions. This exploration can lead to a deeper sense of self-awareness and self-acceptance, helping you build a stronger foundation for your future.

It's important to remember that this process is ongoing and that it's okay not to have all the answers right away. Embrace the opportunity to discover your inner self, and be open to change and grow as you navigate the intricate landscape of your own identity.

This exercise aims to promote self-discovery, self-acceptance, and building self-confidence through positive self-talk.

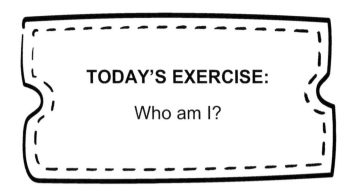

TODAY'S EXERCISE:

Who am I?

Reflect on what makes you who you are. Write down the different aspects of yourself, such as your interests, talents, values, and beliefs. Celebrate the unique combination of these elements that define your self-identity.

Consider how you can explore different parts of yourself and find what feels right for you. Write down activities you can try to discover more about yourself, such as:

EX) Trying new hobbies and activities to see what you enjoy the most.

_____

_____

_____

_____

_____

_____

Practice saying positive things to yourself to boost your self-confidence. Write or draw some positive affirmations you can repeat to yourself, such as:

EX) "I am capable and can achieve my goals."

_____

_____

_____

_____

_____

_____

_____

_____

_____

_____

Reflect on how repeating these positive statements can help you feel more confident and comfortable in your self-identity. Commit to saying them regularly to build a strong sense of self.

_____

_____

_____

_____

_____

_____

_____

_____

_____

_____

_____

DAY 17:

RANDOM ACTS OF KINDNESS

Random acts of kindness are the gentle ripples of compassion that have the power to transform the world. These selfless gestures, often unexpected and spontaneous, carry the immense capacity to brighten someone's day, mend a broken spirit, or even restore one's faith in humanity.

Whether it's holding the door for a stranger, paying a compliment to someone, or simply offering a genuine smile to someone in need, these acts remind us of the beauty of human connection. They transcend barriers of race, religion, and background, reminding us that kindness knows no bounds. In a world that often seems divided and fast-paced, these simple acts serve as a reminder that our shared humanity is a force to be celebrated and cherished.

In this exercise, you'll focus on spreading random acts of kindness to make others smile. You'll explore some ways to do something thoughtful for someone else, such as complimenting a stranger, holding the door open for them, or sending a card in the mail.

This exercise aims to promote empathy, compassion, and positivity by bringing joy to others through small acts of kindness.

TODAY'S EXERCISE:

Let's give some random kindness.

Think about how you can brighten someone's day with a random act of kindness. Write down some ideas, such as:

EX) Send a card or a handwritten note in the mail to someone to show them you care.

- _____

- _____

- _____

- _____

Choose one of the acts of kindness you've written and plan when and where you can do it. **Check with your Mom or Dad that it's safe.**

Take action and perform the random act of kindness. Pay attention to the person's reaction, and notice the positive impact your act of kindness has on them.

Reflect on how spreading kindness made you feel and how it made the other person feel. Write about the experience.

Consider other ways you can continue spreading random acts of kindness in your daily life. Write a list of different ideas you can try in the future.

_____

_____

_____

_____

_____

_____

DAY 18:

PROTECTING YOURSELF FROM NEGATIVITY

You can protect yourself from negativity by forming a strong sense of self-awareness and self-esteem.

It's essential to recognize that negativity often stems from external influences or inner self-doubt. By surrounding yourself with supportive friends and family who uplift you, you can create a positive social circle.

Remember that it's okay to distance yourself from toxic situations and people, prioritizing your mental health and happiness above all else. By taking steps to shield yourself from negativity, you can pave the way for a more positive and fulfilling life.

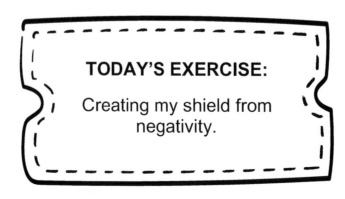

TODAY'S EXERCISE:

Creating my shield from negativity.

Reflect on situations where you've encountered negativity from others. Write down some instances where you felt affected by negative energy.

Consider how you can protect yourself from negativity. Write down different strategies you can use, such as:

EX) Surrounding yourself with positive people: Seek out friends who uplift and support you.

_____

_____

_____

_____

_____

_____

_____

_____

_____

Choose one or more strategies that resonate with you and apply them to your life.

Take note of how these protective measures make you feel and any positive changes you notice.

Reflect on how you can continue protecting yourself from negativity in the future. Write down a plan to maintain your emotional well-being.

MY PLAN

BE KIND
BE BRAVE
BE SILLY
BE HONEST
BE HAPPY
BE YOU

DAY 19:

ESTABLISHING HEALTHY BOUNDARIES

Setting healthy boundaries is essential for maintaining your well-being and fostering healthy relationships.

Boundaries act as a protective shield, defining the limits of what you are comfortable with emotionally, physically, and mentally. They ensure that you prioritize your needs and values, preventing you from overextending yourself or sacrificing your own happiness for the sake of others.

Establishing clear boundaries also aids in effective communication, as it helps others understand your expectations and respect your personal space.

Ultimately, embracing healthy boundaries promotes self-respect and self-care, leading to a more balanced and fulfilling life where you can navigate relationships and situations with confidence and authenticity.

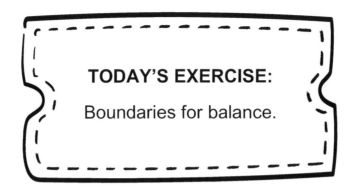

TODAY'S EXERCISE:

Boundaries for balance.

Reflect on areas of your life where you feel the need to set boundaries. Write down situations or relationships where you think establishing boundaries is essential for your well-being.

Consider the different types of boundaries you can set. Write down examples of boundaries you can establish in different situations, such as:

EX) Personal boundaries: Setting limits on what you are comfortable sharing or discussing with others.

EX) Physical boundaries: Respecting your personal space and comfort level with physical touch.

_____

_____

_____

_____

Choose one or more boundaries that you want to set and practice communicating them assertively.

Take note of how setting boundaries affects your well-being and the dynamics of your relationships.

Reflect on how you can continue to maintain healthy boundaries in the future. Write or draw a plan to reinforce and communicate your boundaries effectively.

MY PLAN

DAY 20:

REFLECTING ON YOUR JOURNEY

It's time to reflect on the wonderful journey of self-discovery and growth you've embarked upon. Take a moment to think about all the valuable lessons you've learned, the new skills you've acquired, and the positive changes you've made.

NOW, LET'S TAKE SOME TIME TO REFLECT ON THE PAST 20 DAYS.

Answer the following questions in your workbook:

WHAT WAS YOUR FAVORITE ACTIVITY?

Think about the activities and tasks that you enjoyed the most during this workbook. Why did you like them?

WHAT DID YOU LEARN ABOUT YOURSELF?

Reflect on any new discoveries you made about your strengths, interests, or things you'd like to improve.

_____

_____

_____

_____

_____

_____

_____

_____

_____

_____

WHAT CHALLENGES DID YOU FACE?

Were there any tasks or activities that were challenging for you? How did you overcome them, or what can you do differently next time?

_____

_____

_____

_____

_____

_____

_____

_____

_____

_____

WHAT NEW HABITS HAVE YOU DEVELOPED?

Have you established any new positive habits over the past 20 days? How do they make you feel?

_____

_____

_____

_____

_____

_____

_____

_____

_____

_____

HOW HAS YOUR CONFIDENCE GROWN?

Think about whether you feel more confident now compared to when you started this workbook. Can you pinpoint any specific moments that boosted your self-esteem?

_____

_____

_____

_____

_____

_____

_____

_____

_____

_____

WHAT WILL YOU CARRY FORWARD?

Consider the lessons and skills you've acquired during this journey. Which ones do you want to continue working on in your daily life?

_____

_____

_____

_____

_____

_____

_____

_____

_____

_____

WHO SUPPORTED YOU?

Acknowledge and appreciate the people who supported you throughout this workbook, whether it's your parents, teachers, or friends. How did their support impact your experience?

_____

_____

_____

_____

_____

_____

_____

_____

_____

Always remember, personal growth is a journey that never truly ends.

The skills and wisdom you've gained during our 20-day adventure are the solid foundation upon which you'll build a lifetime of learning and self-improvement. Hold onto this workbook as a cherished keepsake, a map of your incredible journey, and a source of inspiration for those moments when you seek guidance.

You've just taken a remarkable stride towards becoming the best version of yourself. Continue nurturing your personal growth, setting ambitious goals, and having unwavering faith in your own abilities. Your journey is only just beginning, and I want you to know that the horizon is limitless, filled with endless possibilities."

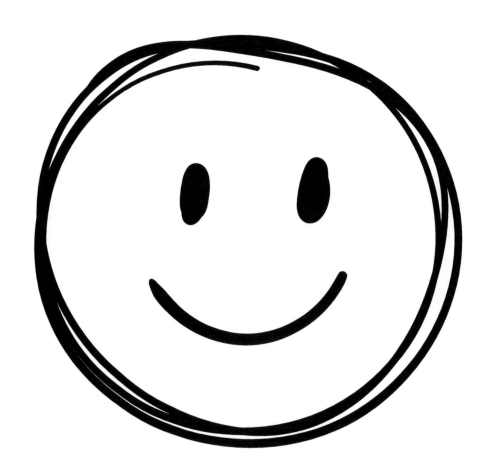

Congratulations on completing the **"Rise Up: Empowering Young Hearts"** journey!

You've taken an incredible first step towards understanding your emotions and empowering yourself to lead a life filled with happiness and confidence.

Remember, your mental health is a lifelong adventure. Understanding your emotions, embracing your true self, and nurturing healthy feelings are ongoing projects that will enrich your life endlessly.

Even though this challenge was for 20 days, I encourage you to keep applying the lessons and ideas from this workbook for the rest of your life.

A special message for our young champs:

Keep those lines of communication open, and always be unapologetically YOU. And never forget to uplift those around you. I know it might seem tough at times, but armed with the right tools and support, you can conquer anything you set your heart on. That includes living a joy-filled life.

BRITTANY HARPER

MOM AND CHILDREN'S MENTAL HEALTH ADVOCATE

DEDICATION

To my daughter Brynlee, You are the inspiration behind these pages, the spark that ignited the creation of this workbook. Watching you navigate the challenges of growing up has shown me the importance of supporting our children through their unique journeys.

To my daughter Arya and son Leland for the love and inspiration you bring into my life every day. Watching you grow and face the challenges of the world has been both a privilege and a source of profound motivation.

To my husband Ryan who has walked every step of this journey with me. I love you.

To all our family and friends for being on his journey with us and supporting us through the emotional rollercoaster we were on and the never ending of support you continue to give us as we get this out to the world.

To Kyle Klymchuk @kyleghostwrites
Your willingness to embark on this unique project brought joy and creativity to the process. Thank you for making this journey both fun and productive, and for translating my ideas onto paper with skill and enthusiasm.

To Holli Snell @hollisnell.va.
Your talent in bringing the vision for the inside of this book to life is truly appreciated. I believe our paths crossed for a reason, and your contribution has added magic to this project.

To every child out there facing similar struggles. May these pages serve as a guide, offering insights and tools to navigate the ups and downs of life. My greatest wish is for you to embrace your authenticity, find happiness, and confidently step into the future.

#BeKind

Printed in Poland
by Amazon Fulfillment
Poland Sp. z o.o., Wrocław

36019529R00060